D0573924

Searchlight BOOKS™

What's Cool
about Science?

Discover

Bionics

Nikole Brooks Bethea

Lerner Publications ◆ Minneapolis

Content Consultant: Gerald E. Loeb, M.D., Professor of Biomedical Engineering, Director of the Medical Device Development Facility, University of Southern California

Lerner Publications Company
A division of Lerner Publishing Group, Inc.
241 First Avenue North
Minneapolis, MN 55401 USA

For reading levels and more information, look up this title at www.lernerbooks.com.

Library of Congress Cataloging-in-Publication Data

Names: Bethea, Nikole Brooks, author.
Title: Discover bionics / by Nikole Brooks Bethea.
Description: Minneapolis : Lerner Publications, [2017] | Series: Searchlight books. What's cool about science? | Audience: Ages 8–11. | Audience: Grades 4 to 6. | Includes bibliographical references and index.
Identifiers: LCCN 2015048771 (print) | LCCN 2015050988 (ebook) | ISBN 9781512408041 (lb : alk. paper) | ISBN 9781512412833 (pb : alk. paper) | ISBN 9781512410624 (eb pdf)
Subjects: LCSH: Bionics—Juvenile literature. | Artificial organs—Juvenile literature. | Prosthesis—Juvenile literature. | Medical innovations—Juvenile literature.
Classification: LCC TA164.2 B48 2017 (print) | LCC TA164.2 (ebook) | DDC 617.9/5—dc23

LC record available at http://lccn.loc.gov/2015048771

Manufactured in the United States of America
1 – VP – 7/15/16

Contents

Chapter 1

WHAT IS BIONICS?

Bionics is the science of combining machines with living things. Bionic devices can help a deaf person hear. They can give a blind person sight. They help injured soldiers walk again. Artificial hearts and kidneys can keep patients alive.

Researchers have made major advances in bionic legs. Besides walking, what else can bionic devices help people do?

People with bionic parts have appeared in science fiction for years. But modern science has brought bionics into real life. People are living better lives thanks to bionic devices.

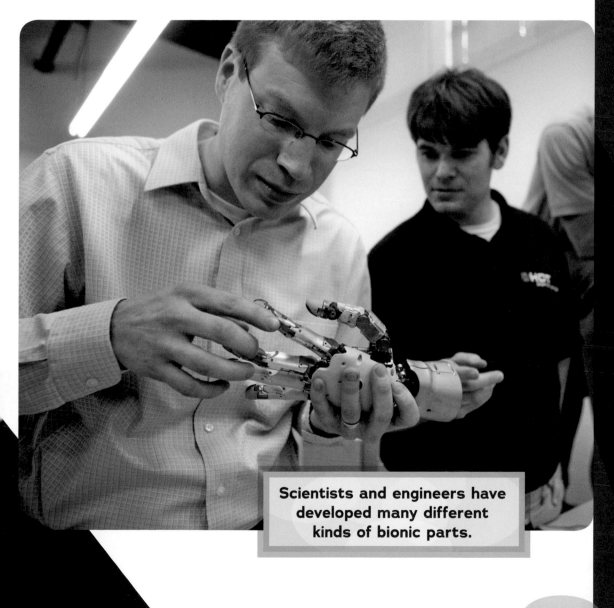

Scientists and engineers have developed many different kinds of bionic parts.

The history of bionics goes back many centuries. Early examples replaced missing body parts. They are called prostheses. Archaeologists found a wooden toe on an Egyptian mummy. It was about 3,000 years old. The toe may have helped the person walk. People built metal hands in the 1500s. The hands let injured soldiers hold swords. They worked using springs and clamps.

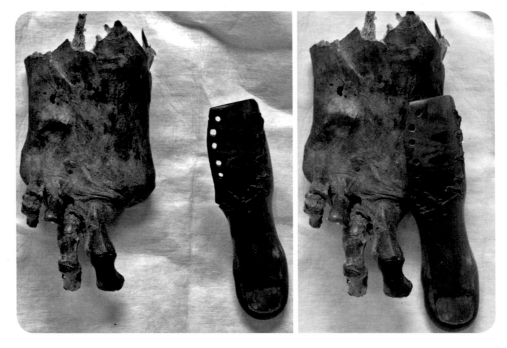

THE EGYPTIAN MUMMY'S PROSTHETIC TOE IS NOW LOCATED AT THE CAIRO MUSEUM IN EGYPT.

With today's specialized prosthetic legs, users can run at high speeds.

These early prostheses were heavy. They were difficult to use. Today's prostheses are much lighter. Plastics replaced wood and metal. Computers make the devices smaller and smarter. They are easier to control.

People use many types of bionics today. Some restore lost body functions. They help people walk or hear. Others replace organs and keep people alive. Cutting-edge bionics will do even more. New technologies will make devices cheaper and better. The future of bionics is looking bright.

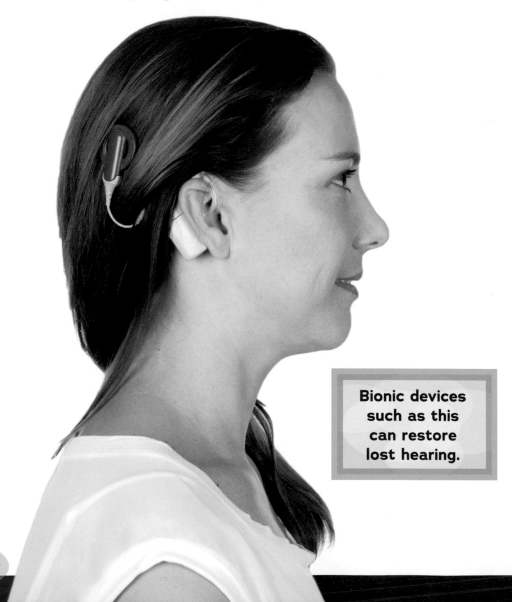

Bionic devices such as this can restore lost hearing.

Building a Bionic Person

Rex is a robot made entirely of bionic parts. His body includes bionic limbs, eyes, and ears. Rex has a mechanical heart that pumps artificial blood. His lungs and kidneys are bionic too. Rex does not have a brain and cannot think. But Rex proves bionics can rebuild much of the human body.

Rex appeared at the Smithsonian National Air and Space Museum in Washington, DC, in 2013.

Chapter 2

RESTORING LOST FUNCTION

Bionic devices help fix or
replace damaged body parts.
People lose limbs from accidents or
from diseases. Today's bionic limbs
are myoelectric. The limb moves by
sensing signals from the person's muscles.

Myoelectric parts
work together with
the body's muscles.
What are two ways
that people might
lose limbs?

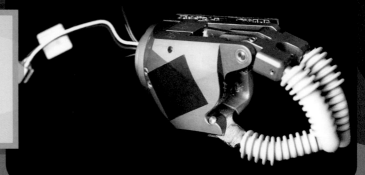

Bionic Arms

Jesse Sullivan has bionic arms. He once worked on power lines. In May 2001, he was shocked while working. His arms were badly damaged. Doctors had to amputate them.

Sullivan (*left*) greets a fellow bionic arm user.

Sullivan has enough control over his arms to complete delicate movements.

Researchers developed a new procedure to help him. They used nerves that once ran to Sullivan's arms. The nerves connect to healthy muscles on his chest. When Sullivan thinks about closing his hand, the muscles in his chest contract. Sensors detect electrical signals from these muscles. The sensors tell the bionic arm to close its hand.

Sullivan's bionic arms have improved his life. They allow him to do everyday tasks himself. He can eat, shave, and put on socks.

Claudia Mitchell, who lost her arm in a motorcycle accident, was the first woman to receive a thought-controlled bionic arm.

Bionic Legs

Many US soldiers in recent wars have had a leg amputated. The army funded research to improve bionic legs. This led to thought-controlled legs. Zac Vawter was the first person to use this new technology. He had been in a motorcycle accident. Vawter lost his right leg from the knee down.

Researchers worked closely with Vawter (*left*) to fit him with the experimental thought-controlled leg.

Researchers used nerves from the damaged muscles in Vawter's right leg. They connected these nerves to healthy muscles above the knee. When Vawter thought about moving the leg, sensors inside it detected signals from the muscle. The sensors told the robotic leg what movement Vawter wanted to make.

IN 2012, VAWTER USED HIS BIONIC LEG TO CLIMB THE STAIRS TO THE 103RD STORY OF WILLIS TOWER IN CHICAGO, ILLINOIS.

In the past, prosthetic legs were remote controlled. Movements were slow. The thought-controlled leg was much easier to use.

Myoelectric limbs, such as this arm in use by a former soldier, are an important part of the future of bionics.

Dancing After Disaster

Adrianne Haslet-Davis was a ballroom dancer. She won awards for her dancing. Her life changed suddenly in April 2013. A bomb exploded near the finish line of the Boston Marathon. It blew part of her foot off. Doctors had to amputate the rest. But Haslet-Davis wanted to dance again. Researchers designed the first bionic leg made for dancing. The bionic leg uses a computer to make complicated movements. In March 2014, Haslet-Davis danced again with her new bionic leg.

Haslet-Davis (*center*) returned to finish the Boston Marathon in 2014.

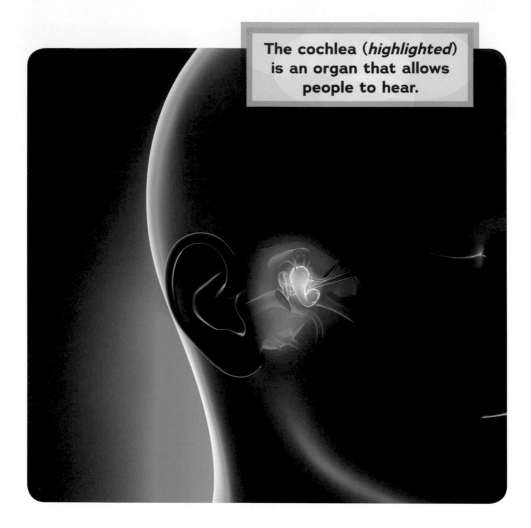

The cochlea (*highlighted*) is an organ that allows people to hear.

Hearing

Bionic devices can also improve a person's senses. A cochlear implant can help deaf people hear. The cochlea is a coiled tube in the ear. It translates sounds into nerve signals. These signals then go to the brain. If the cochlea is damaged, a person can no longer hear.

Cochlear implants go around the damaged part of the ear. Outside the ear are a microphone, speech processor, and transmitter. Surgeons place a receiver and electrodes inside the ear.

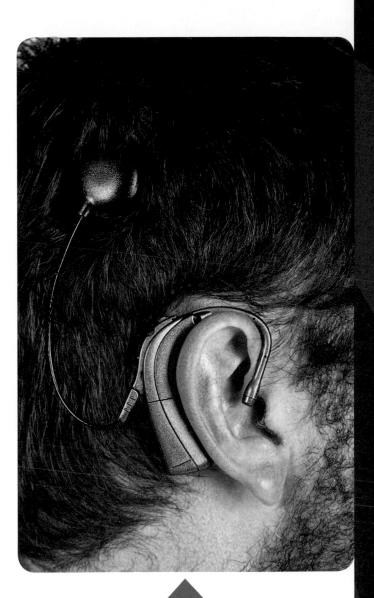

THE MICROPHONE AND SPEECH PROCESSOR HANG AROUND THE EAR, AND THE TRANSMITTER IS ATTACHED TO THE HEAD.

The microphone collects sound from the outside world. The speech processor turns this sound into signals the brain can understand. The transmitter sends these signals through the skin. Here the receiver collects them. Finally, the electrodes pass the signals through the auditory nerve. This nerve sends these signals to the brain. With a cochlear implant, hearing is not completely normal. But it is much better.

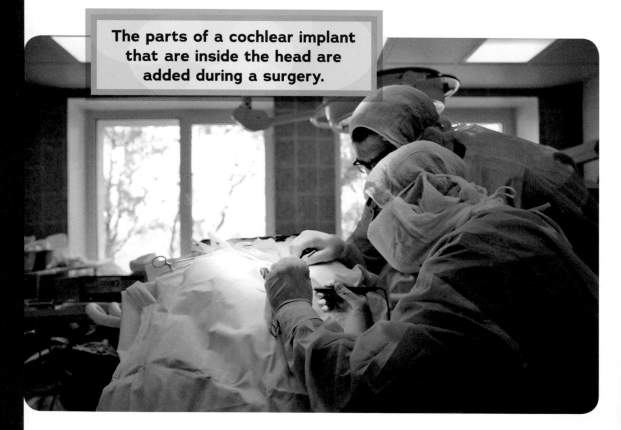

The parts of a cochlear implant that are inside the head are added during a surgery.

Vision

Bionic eye implants can help people with damaged retinas. The retina is in the back of the eye. A healthy retina turns images into electrical signals. The optic nerve sends these signals to the brain. When the retina is damaged, this process does not work.

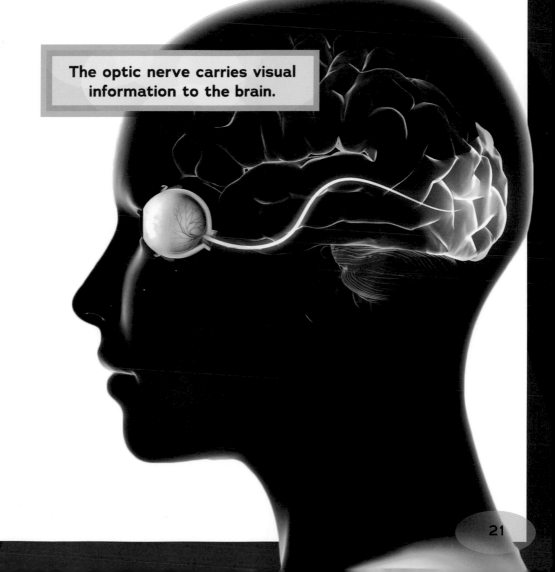

The optic nerve carries visual information to the brain.

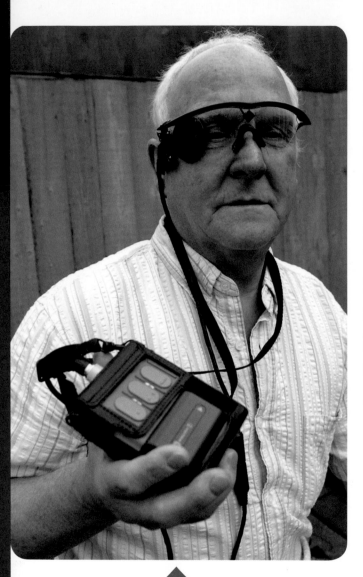

The bionic eye has a video camera attached to a pair of glasses. Users wear a video processing unit. It turns the camera's images into electrical signals. These signals go to an implant in the eye. The optic nerve passes these signals along to the brain.

THIS BIONIC EYE DEVICE IS CALLED THE ARGUS II.

Bionic eyes help people with vision loss travel more easily.

The bionic eye does not restore full vision. Current versions allow the person to tell light from dark. This can help them avoid obstacles. They can tell if a person is in front of them. They can sense curbs and buildings. The eye may not be perfect. However, it is a big improvement. Every year, researchers get closer to giving patients normal functions.

Chapter 3

KEEPING US ALIVE

Bionic devices such as arms and legs can improve a person's life. A person could survive without these devices, but they make life easier. Other types of bionic devices are important for survival. These machines replace organs inside the body.

Artificial hearts have been under development for many years. What is another bionic organ in development now?

Artificial hearts are working inside many people today. Researchers are now developing other bionic organs, such as kidneys. These innovations will save the lives of many patients who might otherwise have died.

The SynCardia artificial heart has been in use since 2004.

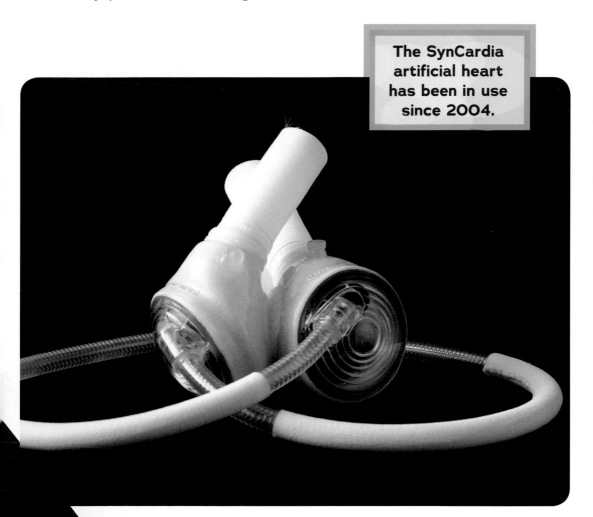

Patients awaiting transplants in hospitals are sometimes connected to large artificial heart machines such as this one.

The Heart

The heart's job is to pump blood through the body. A heart transplant is usually the only cure for heart failure. But the waiting list for donated hearts is very long. Artificial hearts keep people alive while they wait for a heart transplant.

Artificial hearts have mechanical parts that pump blood. Valves control the blood flow. Some artificial hearts connect to a power source outside the body. Others get power from batteries inside the body.

This patient with an artificial heart is wearing a control device (*left*) and a battery (*right*) on his belt.

The Kidneys

Bionic technology can also help people with kidney failure. The kidneys filter waste from blood. The waste leaves the body as urine. When kidneys do not work properly, harmful wastes build up. The usual treatment for kidney failure is dialysis. Patients must go to a clinic several times a week. Blood flows from a patient's body into a machine that filters it.

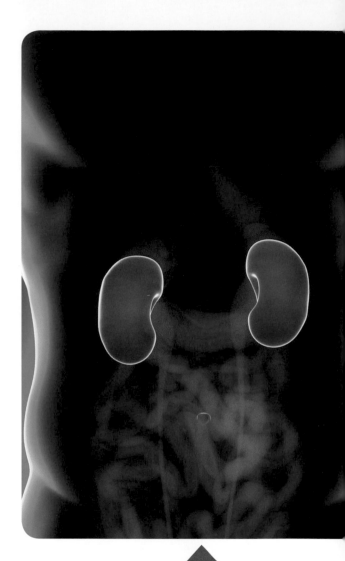

A PERSON HAS TWO KIDNEYS BUT CAN SURVIVE WITH JUST A SINGLE HEALTHY ONE.

Research teams are working on bionic kidneys that can be implanted into the body.

A dialysis machine is the size of a refrigerator. A bionic kidney shrinks this to the size of a coffee cup. The bionic kidney is surgically implanted. Blood goes through a filter in the kidney. Then it flows over a bed of real kidney cells. Here, the blood's salt, sugar, and water levels are balanced. No pump is needed. Blood pressure moves the blood through the artificial kidney.

German researchers have built a miniature version of a human lung in their lab.

Bionic hearts and kidneys are major breakthroughs. But they are only the beginning. Researchers are working on other organs. They include lungs and pancreases. These bionic advances will save many more lives in the decades to come.

Artificial Blood

Researchers at Sheffield University have developed artificial blood. It is made of plastic molecules with an iron core. The blood can carry oxygen through the body. Unlike real blood, it does not have to be cooled when it is stored. This lets it last longer without spoiling. This may be useful in emergencies, such as after earthquakes or hurricanes.

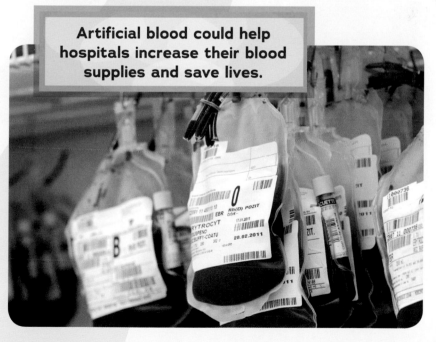

Artificial blood could help hospitals increase their blood supplies and save lives.

Chapter 4

CUTTING-EDGE BIONICS

Today's researchers are working on many new bionic technologies. 3-D printing and brain-implanted computer chips are two areas of study. These advances could make bionics more flexible and powerful than ever before.

This 3-D printer is creating an artificial hand out of plastic. What is another new technology in bionics?

3-D Printing

Many industries now use 3-D printers to make complex parts. 3-D printers create objects layer by layer. People can make custom parts that fit just right. Some researchers are using these printers to build objects from living cells. Someday it may be possible to build bionic devices with living tissue. Printing body parts could open up many new possibilities.

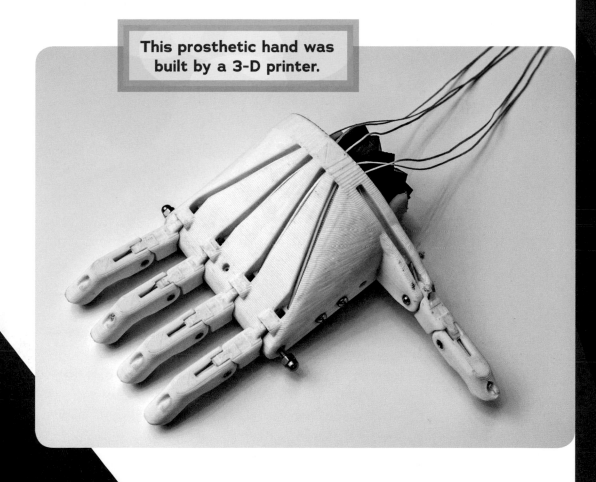

This prosthetic hand was built by a 3-D printer.

Brain Chips

In the future, doctors may implant computer chips in human brains. This could improve function. Scientists have tested a chip to replace damaged brain tissue in rats. The chip repaired damaged memory. It also improved the rats' ability to learn new things.

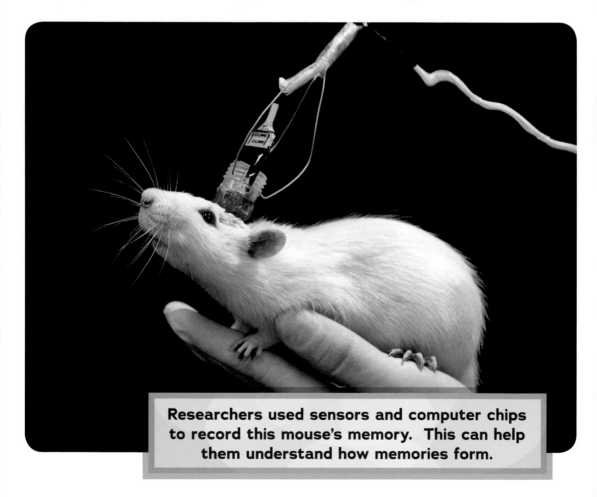

Researchers used sensors and computer chips to record this mouse's memory. This can help them understand how memories form.

Some basic research has also been done on human brain implants. This work could lead to bionic devices that help people with brain damage.

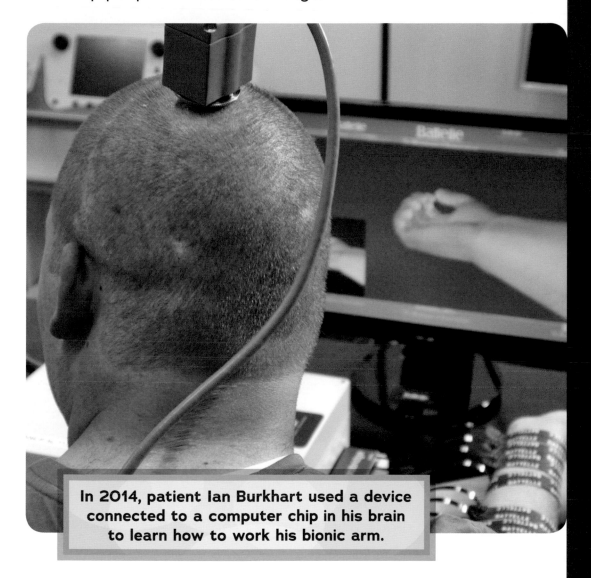

In 2014, patient Ian Burkhart used a device connected to a computer chip in his brain to learn how to work his bionic arm.

Today's bionic devices are tougher and more useful than ever.

Major progress has been made with bionic devices. People are living better lives. They are surviving with bionic organs. The future promises even more amazing advances.

3-D printing could make it cheaper to build bionic devices. This would allow even more people to use them. They could use bionics to walk, hear, or see normally. These possibilities make bionics one of the most exciting fields in science today.

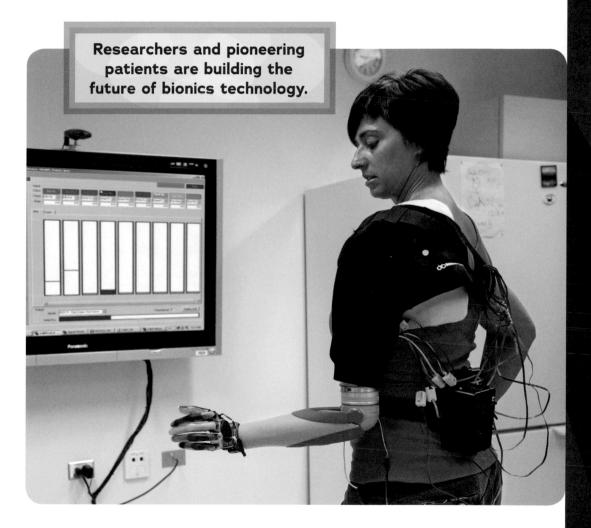

Researchers and pioneering patients are building the future of bionics technology.

Glossary

amputate: to cut off or remove surgically

auditory nerve: a nerve that sends signals from the inner ear to the brain

cochlea: a coiled tube in the inner ear that converts sound vibrations into nerve impulses

dialysis: a medical process that replaces kidney function by removing blood, filtering it, and returning it to the patient

implant: something inserted into a human body

kidney: one of a pair of organs inside the body that remove waste from blood and produce urine

molecule: the smallest unit of a chemical compound, made up of individual atoms

myoelectric: using electrical impulses in muscles to move a bionic part

optic nerve: a nerve that sends signals from the eye to the brain

prosthetic: relating to an artificial body part

Learn More about Bionics

Books

Kenney, Karen Latchana. *What Makes Medical Technology Safer?* Minneapolis, MN: Lerner Publications, 2016. Learn how medical technology, including organ engineering, is keeping people healthy.

Newquist, H. P. *The Human Body: The Story of How We Protect, Repair, and Make Ourselves Stronger.* New York: Viking, 2015. Explore the history of how doctors have fixed and improved the human body.

Woog, Adam. *The Bionic Hand.* Chicago, IL: Norwood House Press, 2010. Discover the history behind one of the world's first bionic hands.

Websites

A History of Prosthetic Devices
http://www.bbc.com/news/health-16599006
See pictures of prosthetic devices throughout history.

How Artificial Hearts Work
http://science.howstuffworks.com/innovation/everyday-innovations/artificial-heart.htm
Read about how artificial hearts perform the functions of real hearts and learn the steps surgeons take when implanting one of these devices.

Jesse Sullivan's Bionic Arms
https://www.youtube.com/watch?v=ddlnW6sm7JE
Watch a video of Jesse Sullivan's bionic arm in action.

Index

Photo Acknowledgments

The images in this book are used with the permission of: © Daily Mail/Rex/Alamy, p. 4; © National Geographic Image Collection/Alamy, pp. 5, 37; © Marwan Naamani/AFP/Getty Images, p. 6; © sportpoint/Shutterstock.com, p. 7; © Elizabeth Hoffmann/iStock.com, p. 8; © epa european pressphoto agency b.v/ Alamy, p. 9; © Universal Images Group North America LLC / Alamy, p. 10; © Matthew Cavanaugh/EPA/Newscom, p. 13; © Jason Reed/Reuters/Newscom, p. 11; © CB2/ZOB/ WENN/Newscom, p. 12; © Brian Kersey/AP Images, p. 14; © John Gress/Reuters/Corbis, p. 15; © Ben Birchall/PA Wire URN:18447735/Press Association/AP Images, p. 16; © CLIPAREA l Custom media/Shutterstock.com, p. 18; © Elsa Hoffmann/Shutterstock.com, p. 19; © Ergin Mikhail/ Shutterstock.com, p. 20; © janulla/iStock.com, pp. 21, 28; © Martin Cleaver/AP Images, p. 22; © Darren Calabrese/The Canadian Press/AP Images, p. 23; © Charles Krupa/AP Images, p. 17; © Jacques Brinon/AP Images, p. 24; © Jeff Topping/Getty Images, p. 25; © Kristyna Wentz-Graff/ MCT/Newscom, p. 26; © Ole Spata/dpa/picture-alliance/Newscom, p. 27; © Peter Yates/Science Source, p. 29; © CB2/ZOB/Supplied by WENN.com/Newscom, p. 30; © Malota/Shutterstock.com, p. 31; © BSIP/Newscom, p. 32; © Timothy Fadek/Corbis, p. 33; © Aly Song/Reuters/Newscom, p. 34; © Lee Powell/The Washington Post/Getty Images, p. 35; © mezzotint/Shutterstock.com, p. 36.

Front Cover: © Jeff J Mitchell/Getty Images.

Main body text set in Adrianna Regular 14/20.
Typeface provided by Chank.